Speak it Believe it LIVE IT

Positive Affirmations for Daily Life
Volume 1

By: Adonica C. Williams

ISBN-13:
978-1719052566

ISBN-10:
1719052565

In loving memory of my mother; Velma Rhea Shackelford. The woman who is responsible for molding me into the woman I am today. Rest easy my queen. Your legacy is strong.

Velma Rhea Shackelford
May 26, 1956-March 5, 2018

Dedication

This book is dedicated to everyone who is determined to live his or her best life. Life has a funny way of turning out, but there are people who refuse to give up, and are always resilient no matter what obstacles may come their way. This book is for you. Never stop learning. Never stop growing. Never stop being your best you!

-Kisses
Adonica

Table of Contents

Day 18: My Marriage will be LIT!
Day 19: I will marry my best friend
Day 20: All of my children will be successful
Day 21: Nobody loves me like I love me
Day 22: My businesses will flourish
Day 23: I will leave a DOPE legacy
Day 24: I am a Warrior
Day 25: I am a Survivor
Day 26: I am NOT a victim. I am a VICTOR
Day 27: When I fall, I will NOT stay down; I will get back up
Day 28: I will NEVER stop trying
Day 29: Every day I will be my best me
Day 30: I will get promoted
Day 31: I choose to be happy
Day 32: I will let God do His job
Day 33: I will sacrifice for what I want
Day 34: I will forgive myself
Day 35: I will NOT be afraid to start over

Introduction

There is so much power in the way you think, and the way you speak. In my almost 40 years of living, I have endured some extremely tumultuous times. As I have grown older, I have learned to find the lesson in everything that happens. Whether the event was good or bad, there is always a lesson to be learned. I decided to write some affirmations to remind myself that no matter what happens, I am in control of my actions. Whatever I think, will be, so I choose to think positive thoughts; even when all I want to do is scream, cry, and complain. I am far from a perfect person, but I *am* in love with my personality, my resilience, my growth, and my attitude towards life. I was dealt some pretty tough cards, and I have stumbled many many times along the way. And because I am still alive, I am sure that I will endure more hard times, and stumble even more; but the one thing I will never do, is quit. I have children, grandchildren, nieces and nephews, and so many other people depending on me that I simply cannot fail. I truly believe I was put on this earth to help and encourage people, make people smile, and show love and kindness to others. I also believe that the obstacles I have faced have shaped me into the strong individual I am today. I can help so many other people now, because I have been through so many things. No one will ever be able to tell by looking at me, and that's exactly the way I want it. I enjoy being the shoulder to cry on, the listening ear, and the words of encouragement to those who confide in me. Please note, you may not agree with all of these affirmations. That is quite fine. In life we have the choice to keep what we want, and discard what we don't. However, I pray that these words of affirmation will encourage someone in some way.

Day 1

Today I will start

Whether you are starting for the first time or starting over…again. Today is your day to start. Too many times we make plans to be great only to have those plans overlooked or put on hold. We are always saying we will start tomorrow, or next week or even next year. Well today I urge you to carry out just one goal or plan that you have been wanting to complete. That business you want to launch…Start! That blog you want to write…Start! That diet or lifestyle change you want to try…Start! Do it. Live unapologetically. Do what makes you happy. If you've been meaning to stand up for yourself and stop letting people walk all over you, now is the time. If you've been meaning to mend that broken relationship or friendship, today is the day. Make today your day you start whatever it is you've been putting off; or just start something new!

Day 2

The breakup was not my fault

A breakup doesn't always have to be a romantic relationship breakup. There are times we break up with friends, or associates as they may be. We break up with jobs (quit or fired). Sometimes we even break up with our kids (for a little while). Maybe a business venture with someone didn't work out. No matter who it was or what it was, something didn't work out. Even if you think you were the blame for whatever the breakup was; or you may have even BEEN the blame; ultimately it's still not your fault. I believe everything that happens in my life is divinely orchestrated by God. So if something does not work out, that means that I am being set up for something even greater to happen. So if something in your life did not work out and you had to part ways with someone, it's ok. Everything happens for a reason. Learn your lesson, trust the process and know that greater is coming.

Day 3

I am worthy of true love

Say this to yourself. Believe it! Don't let anybody tell you otherwise. You are worthy of all the love your heart can hold. Your true love comes in many forms. My true love has come from my children, my family, my friends, and my future husband. I was once told by an ex that no one would want me after him and that I would be forever alone. I laughed at that foolishness. Because God has given me much too much of true love. And I'll never be alone. If you are discouraged about finding true love or your true love finding you, pick your head up right now and stop that. Focus on the love you already have. Love yourself truly. Love the people that love you truly. Give love and love will come. You are worthy. You always have been.

Day 4

I will NOT let a breakup break me

Chins up! Crowns straightened! Whatever left...let it go! Friends, mates, situations, or positions. If it passed, that simply means it wasn't yours to keep. Everyone comes in to your life to teach you something. To make you stronger. To help you be a better you. Yeah you may help them in the process but when their time is up in your life you have to let them go. Some will stay a lifetime, but some will leave. What you can NOT do is fall off and stay sad forever. Don't let anything break you. Use your pieces to build a better you. Pray! Cry! Regroup! Learn from the experience, even bend if you have to. But whatever you do...don't break! You're royalty. You've got this!

Day 5

I forgive my Ex(s)

I know this is a tough one but it has to be said and it has to be done. Whoever your ex is, you have to forgive them. Ex-colleague, Ex-friend, Ex-lover, Ex…whoever. You may have been the victim. You may have been wronged. How dare they treat you like that? And you're absolutely right; they shouldn't have done whatever they did. But guess what? Those people are somewhere living while you are a prisoner of your own "should have beens." They "should have" done this or they "should have" done that. Welp! They didn't. It's time for you to forgive whoever for doing whatever. This frees you from you! This frees you from THEM having any more power over your thoughts and actions. This frees up space in your heart to receive the gestures and gifts from someone who WILL treat you the right way. And just because you forgive them, doesn't mean you have to be their friend, it just means you let go of the hurt. When you let go, you'll have so much room for good stuff. Some of us can't receive our good stuff because our hands are too full with unforgiveness. There's no room for the good. Man drop that junk! I know it's hard, but you have to forgive…for your own sanity. Let go of what hurt you. Let go of who hurt you. But never forget what it taught you. Learn from the experience, forgive the situation and live your life. Because there's nothing like a good ole forgiveness Boss up!

Day 6

I embrace new opportunities with a clean and open heart

Psalm 51:10 says, "Create in me a clean heart and renew a right spirit within me." Whatever you are doing that is new, embrace it with genuine newness. Don't bring any old baggage into the new. The new job, the new friendship, the new business, the new relationship. Give them all a fresh clean chance to work out for your good. Starting fresh means leaving old things behind. The hurt, the negativity, the garbage, the naysayers; whatever it was that didn't work before, leave it!! When building a new foundation, if you bring baggage from the past, you are sure to build the same house. I don't know about you, but I want fresh NEW bricks to build my mansion! Free yourself from the past and embrace the new anew. Love like you've never been hurt. Try like you've never failed. Work like you've never had to. Don't think about what won't work, just focus on what will. "But what if I fall?"...Oh but sweetie, what if you fly?!

Day 7

I will let God lead my path

Let me be the first to say this…I do not run my own life. Simply because I have no idea what I am doing. I consult God daily, hourly, sometimes minutely, because I want things to go right. Ask God to direct you and trust that He will do just that. Your path will not always be a pleasant and easy one. But if you know that God is leading then trust that the difficult and unpleasant will teach you and help you grow and eventually lead you to your blessings, your breakthrough, your peaks. God also uses us to help others. And sometimes you have to have "been" there to help someone else who is going through what you've been through. It can be so difficult when you don't know what tomorrow brings, when you have no control over what will happen next, or even when you have plans for your life and they are abruptly altered. Trust me, I speak from experience. But surrender that control to God and let him lead you. You won't regret it. You'll cry, you'll hurt, you'll even want to question

God; but when you come out on top, you'll look back at all the trials and thank Him for leading your path.

Day 8

I will consult God before making any decisions

This is a continuation from yesterday. So many times we want to just do what we want to do and not think about the consequences of our actions. Then, when stuff blows up in our face, we want to run to God for solace and help. Everything is not the devil…sometimes we mess our own selves up. We are all guilty of it. However, when we consult God before making our decisions, and not move so hastily; things tend to turn out better. Talk to God. Consult with God. Ask God if what you are doing is the right thing. He has a funny way of telling you yes or no. When things don't work out right before you were going to make a move, that's God's protection. When things go exactly as planned and even smoother than you thought, that's God's approval. You have to have your own relationship with God though; an intimate relationship. You can't just put God on a shelf, not pay Him any attention, and take him down when you need Him. This relationship is continuous. So, whatever you are planning on doing, consult God first. Then use your discernment. He listens, and He moves on your behalf.

Day 9

People Love Me

That's right…they do! So many times you focus so much on who doesn't like you or who doesn't approve of you that you forget that there are a plethora of people who love you just the way you are; flaws and all. It's in people's nature to want to be liked by all. Even the ones who swear all the time that they don't care; inside, they really do. Nobody wants to admit they think that but it's true. So you tend to zero in on the one person who you think does not see how good a person you are because you want them somehow to be convinced that you are likeable. You want that 100%. NEWSFLASH! It's not going to happen. No matter what you do, someone will not like you. So you have to live your life and love the ones who love you. You can even love the ones who don't like you. You don't have to fool with them though. Believe it or not, some people don't like me. But so many people do that it no longer bothers me who doesn't. It used to, but not anymore. Those people aren't paying any of my bills anyway. It's not just children who struggle with this; some adults do as well. Well, that all ends today. From here on out, your job is to only focus on the people who love you. The people who know you. The people who don't want to live without you. Because I promise if you lined up the people who love you with the people you think don't care for you, the love line would be FAR greater than the latter. So love yourself, shift your focus to the people that love you, and don't give any more thoughts, time, or energy to the people who don't. You don't have to confess or admit it; and if this message doesn't pertain to you that's fine. But to the people who it touches, please know this…You are amazing! Stay that way! I love you!

Day 10

I will always make sure God comes first

Our lives get so busy at times that we often forget about God until something happens and we need Him. We spend so much time on our families, careers, friends, and just our own lives, that God often has to get in where HE fits in. We have to sit back, evaluate, and reposition God in our lives. Be honest with yourself…how often do you start your day with scripture and prayer? And no, not the quick prayer you pray on the way to work, or reciting the 23rd Psalm. But really put a little time aside to have an intimate connection with God. Growing up I've always been told that God is a jealous god. He doesn't want anything put before Him. As an adult, I think of how jealous I am about certain things. I don't like the way I feel when I feel like I'm being put on the back burner. God feels the same way. So let's do better by the one who gives us everything in spite of us deserving it or even needing it. The one who spoils us rotten and forgives us time and time again, no matter how badly we mess up. Put God at the head and everything else will fall into place.

Day 11

I will continuously chase my dreams

Never stop chasing your dreams. Whatever you thought of, whatever you started, whatever you wanted to do that you put on the back burner in order to live your life day to day...today is the day to go back and pick them back up. Do what makes you happy. Write that blog. Start that business. Sell that tea. Sell those waist trainers. Go and volunteer. Give back to your community. Get that degree. Go back to school. Buy that house. Do whatever you planned to do. Those dreams aren't going to pursue themselves. Trust me. You've got this! Do your thing. Go ahead and be great! I'm rooting for you!

Day 12

I will focus only on the positive

People will tell you that I'm one of the most positive and optimistic people they know. I try real hard to be that way. But it's so much easier said than done when it feels like all hell is breaking loose. But in every bad situation, you can always find some good. Try to focus on the positive in everything that comes your way. What you feed is what will grow. Feed your mind positive vibes. Train your mind to find some good in everything, every day. I have challenged myself to do this and I challenge you all to do it as well. You will have your moments, and that's ok, but don't stay upset for too long. Find some good and try to be positive! Have a wonderful Day!

Day 13

I will NOT become bitter

Whatever you do, don't be bitter. Whatever didn't work out; whatever didn't go your way…accept what is and keep moving. Find the positive and hold on to that. It's so easy to be the victim and cry, "woe is me." It's also easy to use pain as an excuse to be mean and nasty to other people. Please don't be bitter. Pray for yourself and ask God to heal your heart and deliver you from whatever it is that hurt you. Don't waste time being bitter…spend your time being sweet. Keep sweetness in your heart and let it flow through no matter what. Never walk around with a frown, you never know who's falling in love with your smile.

Day 14

I will love again

Short…Sweet…Simple. You *will* love again. You *will* love your job again. You *will* love your passion again. You *will* have relationship love again. You *will* love YOURSELF again! Keep your heart open and receptive to love again. Whatever love you desire is what you will have. Waking up happy to go to do a job you love, *will* happen. Waking up working at your dream come true, *will* happen. Waking up to faces that you love, *will* happen. Waking up next to the person you love, *will* happen. Waking up in the city you love, *will* happen. Believe in love…it always comes back around.

Day 15

I thank God for protecting me from bad relationships

Hear me and hear me good. Sometimes God allows things to happen for your protection. Ya'll broke up because God knew that person would be a terrible spouse to you if ya'll got married. You got that divorce because that first marriage was trial and error (LOL) and God knew He had a REAL spouse just for you, had you just been patient. You lost that job because God knew that you needed to start your own business. You lost that friend because God knew that HE was taking you higher and that friend was stunting your growth. Detachment is extremely painful sometimes, but trust that there is a reason for the cut off. God, I thank you for your protection! Think about something you thought you couldn't live without…now look at you; out here living without it…like a Boss!

Day 16

I am Strong, Attractive, and Confident

Speak it! Believe it! Live it! Too many of you have lost yourself *in* yourself. You've been feeling weak, overwhelmed, mentally tired, and just not feeling like yourself. Get your fire back! Tap into your inner strengths and let them shine through. Find that confidence that you have buried deep inside of your fears and bring it out. Know that you are attractive and amazing and let that light shine. Be bold! Be Confident! Be strong! I know you can. Today is a day to *"feel"* yourself! Go on Kings and Queens…Feel Yourself! Slay on!

Day 17

My future spouse will appreciate me and show it

This isn't a word for everybody. It's a word for who it's a word for. If you still believe in love and marriage. If you're waiting on God to bless you with your spouse; then this is for you. Speak it, think it, believe it! When you get your spouse, they will *not* be the one who doesn't show you how much they love and appreciate you. There will be no games. There will be no puzzles. You will be shown the love and appreciation that you dish out. Wait on God, and when your spouse comes, treat them with the same love and appreciation you want to be shown and you both will be great! I'm rooting for you!

Day 18

My Marriage will be LIT!

Life is what you make it. Therefore, so is your marriage. If you want a fun and exciting marriage...make it that way...keep it that way. Coming home to your best friend. Worshipping with the one you love. Raising the kids. Taking trips. Netflixing. Shopping. Building together. Stacking together. Walking in to the future together. Working through differences together. That person that you can't wait to talk to when something happens. Yeah. That's LIT. It can happen. Don't let anyone tell you it can't. The choice is yours. I plan to be the BOMB wife! Watch your marriage be LIT! I'm rooting for you.

Day 19

I will marry my best friend

To be in love is one thing. But to be in love with a person that you actually LIKE is another. Meet your best friend. Become best friends. Date your best friend. Marry your best friend. How amazing would it be to be married to the person that you always want to talk to, always want to be around; the one you can tell anything and your secret is safe. The one who won't judge you when you fall; but would rather pick you up. But also the one who will keep it real and put you back on the right track. That's a best friend for you. Why wouldn't you want your spouse to be that same person? Of course you will have your own friends. But after all those years of being married, I would just like to still "like" the person I'm married to. Friendship is amazing. I'm going to marry my best friend; just watch and see (speaking into existence).

Day 20

All of my children will be successful

Say it! Believe it! Do your absolute best as a parent and leave the rest up to the children and God. I have children and I claim success over each of their lives daily. Speak success over your children. Pray for your children. Talk to your children. Teach your children. And most importantly SUPPORT your children. My oldest son wanted to be a Power Ranger when he was younger. He wanted to help people. I wasn't having it. But my mother supported the Power Ranger dream 100%. Eventually he grew out of it but he's still one of the kindest souls you'll ever meet. So he's still helping others just like he wanted to do. There will be some bumps along the way, but stand by them as they find their way to success. Help them through school. Help them with that business plan. Buy their product. Do whatever you can to support their dreams. Be their biggest cheerleader and their biggest supporter. Your children will be successful. You, as a parent, will see to it!

Day 21

Nobody loves me like I love me

People spend so much time loving other people and showing others how much they love them. Make sure you take just as much time if not even more, to love yourself. Cut anything out of your life that doesn't contribute to your happiness. Cut anything that isn't contributing to your personal growth. You don't owe anybody any explanations. It's all a part of loving yourself first and foremost. You can't pour from an empty cup, and people will take as long as you're giving. Take care of you. Love on you. Be proud of you. Cheer for you. Encourage you. Give your own self advice. Make YOU your #1 Fan! Make sure you love yourself for YOU and do an awesome job of it. U.G.L.Y. is one of my favorite acronyms. U Gotta Love Yourself. I was taught this acronym in college and I live by it every day. It's ok to love yourself. It'll help you spread love to others.

Day 22

My businesses will flourish

Dream. Follow. Pursue. Whatever you want to do, go ahead and get it done. Whatever business you want to start will be successful. Whatever book you want to write will be a best seller. Whatever cause you want to support will be heard and supported. Whatever you want to create and sell will sell. There's enough money out here for everybody. There's enough bread out here for all of us to eat. Buy that property. Start that business. Create that foundation. Write that blog. Write that book. Finish whatever you started. It's time to be successful. We will all flourish together! Let's get this success and leave these Legacies! I'm rooting for you.

Day 23

I will leave a DOPE legacy

This is a continuation from yesterday. You will be successful and you will also leave a magnificent legacy! Your legacy includes your lessons you teach your children. Your legacy includes how well you treated people. Your legacy includes your humanitarianism. Your legacy includes the vacations, the trips, the nights you and your babies popped popcorn and watched TV together. The game nights. The pep talks. The encouragement. The scolding. It includes your way of life. When I'm long gone, I want the memories of me to be good enough for people to smile. I want my children to be able to say I taught them well. I want my businesses to keep flourishing long after I'm gone. I want the legacy I leave to be dope! You will leave a dope legacy too! I just know you will! I love ya'll!

D.O.P.E.
Driven. Optimistic. Persistent. Educated

Day 24

I am a Warrior

A warrior is defined as a brave or experienced soldier or fighter. Is that NOT what you are? You fight your way through life every day and you do it well. No matter what it may seem like you always come out on top. That's because you're amazing. That's because you're a fighter. That's because you're a warrior! Keep fighting. Never stop. Never give up. You're the best! You're a warrior!

Day 25

I am a Survivor

Life has thrown so much your way. You have suffered, endured, and triumphed time and time again. Remember that time you were so broken and so hurt that you didn't know how you were going to get back to happy? You survived that. You have survived losses of loved ones, lost jobs, lost friendships, lost relationships. You have survived being mistreated, lied on, passed over, pushed aside. You have been knocked down, but you never stayed there. You have endured so much hurt and disappointment; and in the end you have always stood tall! That victorious attitude and non-wavering tenacity is why no matter what storms blow your way, you always survive. Keep smiling Sunshine…you're a survivor! Say it. Believe it. Live it!

Day 26

I am NOT a victim.
I am a VICTOR

You are Victorious! When faced with challenges you will be the victor. No matter what life throws at you, don't worry, you will be victorious over everything. You are *not* a victim. You have strength and power. You will always be the victor. It may look like you're losing, but keep the faith and you will soon see that you will once again come out on top. God loves you too much to leave you all alone. This is why you will always win. Keep the faith, stay the course, and trust the process. With God, you will ALWAYS be the Victor! Have a great day DIVAs!!!!

D.I.V.A.

Divine Individual Victorious & Anointed

Day 27

When I fall, I will NOT stay down; I will get back up

Speak it! Believe it! Live it! Peaks and valleys. Sunshine and rain. We fall down but we get up. These are all some sayings that keep us going. Life throws us all kinds of curve balls. Sometimes they miss us, sometimes they graze us, and sometimes they knock us clean down. But the great thing about us all is, we always get back up. Whatever it is that has recently knocked you down? Go ahead and get back up. Crawl if you have to. Duck walk if you have to. Army crawl if you have to. But never stay still. Soon you'll be back on your feet and better than ever. I believe this. So whatever you do, don't you stay down too long. I'm rooting for you!

Day 28

I will NEVER stop trying

Obstacles come every day and in every way. But you never stop. You keep trying no matter what. You wake up every day and you try. You try to live better. You try to eat right. You try to attain your body goals. You try to be a good parent. You try to reach your goals. You try to stay close to God. You try to stay positive in spite of being surrounded by negativity. Don't stop trying. You will continue to achieve. You will continue to rise. Trying is what keeps you going. And by always trying, you always succeed. Whatever you do…DON'T Stop! Keep Trying! I'm rooting for you!

Day 29

Every day I will be my best me

Say it! Believe it! Live it! Every day you wake up you get to make a choice. Some people choose to be sour. Some people choose to be happy. Some people wake up with a burning excitement and ready to take the day on. Yesterday is gone. Try not to dwell too much on whatever happened the day before unless it's helping you improve. Is it making you a better you? Is it growing you? Is it maturing you? If not, then trash it and start fresh. The great thing about being yourself is the fact that you get to choose what you will and will not react to. However you decide to start your day...be your best at it. Focus on your goals. Recite your affirmations. Save your money. Work on your credit. Complete that vision board...then that vision! I'm my happiest when I'm being my best me. Wake up every day with the determination to be your best you. You can do it. I'm rooting for you.

Day 30

I will get promoted

Promote means: Further the progress of something or to support or actively encourage. It also means to advance or raise someone to a higher position or rank. This is not just in reference to a job. This is in reference to every facet of your life. Your relationship will be elevated. Your marriage will progress. Your goals will be supported. Your esteem will rise. Your children will advance. Girlfriends are being promoted to wives. Friends are being promoted to family. Small businesses are being promoted to bigger businesses. Employees are being promoted to bosses. Self-love is being promoted daily. Your life will be LIT! Get ready for your promotions. Mind, Body, Soul, Spirit and all other areas.

Day 31

I choose to be happy

Your attitude is your choice. No matter what comes your way, your reactions and attitude are up to you. You can't always control what happens to you, but you CAN control how you react. You also have the power to choose your attitude in any situation. Choose happiness. Choose optimism. Choose to smile. Choose goodness. Choose to breathe and walk away. Choose to hang up. Choose to block negativity. It won't always be easy, but keep practicing and with time it will get easier. The power of life and death is in the tongue. Speak it! Believe it! Live it! I'm rooting for you…With your Happy Self!

Day 32

I will let God do His job

I'm not the only one who is guilty of this. Trying to "help" God do His work in my life. Our job is to sit back, trust the process, and let God work. So many times we say we will pray and don't worry. But the human in us always wants to "control" some part of the process or "know" the end before God makes His reveal. Patience is hard sometimes. But we *must* let God work. We trust the process. But sometimes we just want the process "hurried up." We will LET God do His job. We will remain faithful to His word. We will continue to be patient. And we will ultimately prosper. Favor isn't fair but when it's your time nothing or no one can stop it!

Day 33

I will sacrifice for what I want

Everybody wants something. Whether it be a new business, a marriage, children, a new job, saving money, or whatever it is you desire. With every goal there is going to have to be some sacrifice. You won't get what you want without giving up something you already have. It could be something as simple as time. You may have spent all of your weekend time binge watching shows. But since you started your new business you have to spend your weekends planning and bookkeeping. It could be saving money for a down payment on a new car, but you LOVE to shop for shoes (guilty). So guess who has to stop buying shoes in order to drive that new ride? Yeah…you can't drive a shoe…you can walk though LOL… If it's a child you want, trust me you will sacrifice a lot…mostly just sleep; but the trade-off is well worth it. Whatever it is you want to do...DO IT! Just know that it will come with some sacrifices. Be ok with making the sacrifices for now, because in the long run the sacrifices will be well worth it. What will you sacrifice for what you really want?

Day 34

I will forgive myself

Everybody has done something or said something that they wish they wouldn't have. Too many people are walking around pretending to be perfect but dying inside. Well...I'm here to tell you that it's ok. Mistakes is how we grow. Mistakes is how we learn. Mistakes humble us. Forgive yourself for your bad choices. Forgive yourself for ignoring your intuitions and falling flat on your face because of it. Stop beating yourself up. It's ok. Life goes on and if you want it to life gets better. Forgive yourself and learn from your mistakes and bad choices. Forgive yourself for holding those grudges. Turn your regrets into power. Who knows, maybe your story will inspire others. But you can't be an inspiration if you're constantly wallowing in self-pity. It's okay. Forgive yourself.

Day 35

I will NOT be afraid to start over

Let me tell you something…START OVER! Don't let nobody talk you into staying in no kind of situation that you don't want to be in. You hate that job? Start over! Relationship not working out? Start over! Started your dream then got distracted? Start over! Fell off with your Walk with Christ? Start over! Gained that weight back? Start Over! Start over as many times as you need, to get it right. Years mean nothing if you're unhappy. When you close your eyes at night, the only person that you have to be pleased with is yourself. So if you've got to start over…do just that! You owe nobody an explanation for ANY decisions you make regarding YOUR LIFE! Do you! Be happy…START OVER!

This area was designed to help you take notes and write some of your own affirmations. What are some things you want to accomplish and how will you accomplish them? You've got this. I'm rooting for you. -Adonica

About The Author

Adonica Williams was born and raised in Orlando, Florida. She has been an educator for more than a decade. She graduated from Jones High School and Bethune-Cookman College. As a child she often wrote as a means to express herself as opposed to talking; and has had a vivid imagination since she was three years old. Adonica's goal is to write as many books as she can and touch as many lives as possible before her time on earth is expired.

Other titles:
These Fools Be Lying
Passion, Pain, & Perseverance

Stay connected to Adonica Williams:
www.mschontel.weebly.com

Facebook:
MschontelWrites
MsChontel

Instagram:
@AdonicaIsms

Made in the USA
Middletown, DE
10 April 2024

52797412R00031